TRACKING DOWN
ANGLO-
SAXONS
IN BRITAIN

TRACKING DOWN
ANGLO-
SAXONS
IN BRITAIN
MOIRA BUTTERFIELD
W
FRANKLIN WATTS
LONDON•SYDNEY

First published in 2010 by Franklin Watts

Franklin Watts
338 Euston Road
London NW1 3BH

Franklin Watts Australia
Level 17/207 Kent Street
Sydney, NSW 2000

A CIP catalogue record for this book is available from the British Library.

Dewey number: 942'.01

ISBN 978 0 7496 9233 9

Printed in China

Franklin Watts is a division of Hachette Children's Books, an Hachette UK company.

www.hachette.co.uk

Editor: Sarah Ridley
Design: John Christopher/White Design
Editor in Chief: John C. Miles
Art director: Jonathan Hair

Picture credits:
AJD Photo/Alamy: 24tl. Ashmolean Museum, Oxford/Bridgeman Art Library: 23. Krys Bailey/Alamy: 25t. ©The British Library Board. All Rights Reserved 2009. Cotton Tiberius B.I, f 144 v.: 25b. © The Trustees of the British Museum: 13bl, 13tr. Cols Churches/Alamy: 27t. Alan Crawford/istockphoto: front cover, 9tr. Rob Estall/Alamy: 29b. The Granger Collection/Topfoto: 12. Roger Howard/PD: 8. Interfoto/Alamy: 29t. Michael Jenner/Alamy: 27b. Terry Matthews/Alamy: 26. John Miller/Alamy: 6. John Morrison/Alamy: 14b. Musée de la Tapisserie, Bayeux, France/Bridgeman Art Library: 7. Picturepoint /Topham: 9cl. The Portable Antiquities Scheme. CC: 16t, 16cr, 16b, 17c, 30b. Paul Rumsey: 22. St Paul's Jarrow: 19t. Peter Scholey/Alamy: 14t, 15. Skyscan/Alamy: 10. Topfoto: 11, 17b. Travelshots/Alamy: 28. The Master & Fellows of University College, Oxford: 18. Courtesy of West Stow: 20-21, 21r. © 2009 Winchester City Council: 9bl, 24b. Adam Woolfit/Corbis: 19b. *Every attempt has been made to clear copyright. Should there be any inadvertent omission please apply to the publisher for rectification.*

CONTENTS

ALL ABOUT THE ANGLO-SAXONS

In 410CE the Roman army left Britain. The Romans had ruled for 400 years, but fierce warriors were beginning to attack their empire, including Britain. Some of these new arrivals eventually settled in England and became known as the Anglo-Saxons.

Land-snatchers

The warriors came from Germany, Denmark and Holland to seize land for themselves. They were called the Angles, the Saxons and the Jutes. Eventually they settled in south, southwest and northern England, creating several new mini-kingdoms with local rulers. We don't know much about this time in English history, but we do know it was violent and there were lots of battles as the local Britons tried to stop the invaders.

← Reculver in Kent, a spot where invaders may once have attacked from abroad. An Anglo-Saxon monastery (now in ruins) was eventually built on the site of the old Roman fort.

Anglo-Saxons v. Vikings

In the 8th century some bloodthirsty new invaders, the Vikings, arrived from Norway, Sweden and Denmark, looking for new lands. They took half of England for themselves, killing the local Anglo-Saxon rulers. The Anglo-Saxon king, Alfred of Wessex, finally stopped their advance. The Vikings were gradually driven back, and in 927CE Alfred's grandson Athelstan became the first ever ruler of the whole of England.

↑ Harold, the last Anglo-Saxon king, is crowned (see page 29).

Death of a king

The Anglo-Saxons were finally defeated by the Normans at the Battle of Hastings in 1066. Harold, the last Anglo-Saxon king, was killed, and William of Normandy took over the country. His French forces drove out the Anglo-Saxon nobles and took their lands, but the ordinary Anglo-Saxon villagers carried on their everyday lives under the new Norman lords.

ANGLO-SAXON PEOPLE

When Anglo-Saxon invaders arrived in England, they split the land they conquered into several different kingdoms ruled by local kings. Every Anglo-Saxon promised 'fealty', loyalty, to his king.

Kings and warriors

There were strict ranks in the Anglo-Saxon world. The most important person was the king, followed by his nobles, the eoldermen. Then came the thanes, the warriors in his army. An Anglo-Saxon king was more like a local warlord than a modern king. It was a dangerous position because it was a violent time in English history, and if a king lost a battle, his enemies would usually execute him.

← This statue of King Alfred – one of the most successful Anglo-Saxon kings – stands in Winchester (see pages 22-25).

LOOK FOR

Anglo-Saxon Treasures

Here are some typical finds which help archaeologists to identify places where Anglo-Saxons lived.

Anglo-Saxon coins
Anglo-Saxons dropped coins, just as we do today. The coins were often marked with the reigning king's profile or name. We can work out the date of the coin from the markings.

Burial sites
Anglo-Saxons were often buried with objects such as jewellery and weapons.

Church manuscripts
Anglo-Saxon poems and stories were written down by monks of the time.

Freedmen and slaves

The next rank down was that of the freedmen – farmers and craftsmen who lived in villages with their families and owned their own land. The king could call up the freedmen to fight in his army, if he needed them. Beneath the freedmen were slaves – prisoners-of-war or the very poor, who worked on the land. Some of these slaves may well have been captured Britons.

➔ The ruins of the monastery at Lindisfarne, an important religious centre in Anglo-Saxon times.

➔ Anglo-Saxon coins, marked with a cross and the name of the king.

Writing monks

Soon after the Anglo-Saxons conquered England they became Christian and began to build monasteries and churches. Monks were the only people at that time who learnt to read and write. They copied out the Bible by hand and wrote down poems and histories. Some of their writing survives to tell us about Anglo-Saxon life.

➔ A beautiful hanging bronze bowl found in the grave of a young Anglo-Saxon man buried near Winchester.

LAST STAND OF THE BRITS

The invading Anglo-Saxons pushed the native Britons back into Wales, Cornwall and Cumbria in the north, but they didn't win without a fight. We don't know exactly what happened, but it's thought that battles took place around British hilltop fortresses, such as the remains shown here at South Cadbury in Somerset.

Bad move?

Nobody wrote down the story of the Anglo-Saxon invasion at the time. We only have histories written hundreds of years later. One of these tells how, in the 5th century, a British king of Kent called Vortigern paid Anglo-Saxon warriors to come and help him fight off raiders. The hired fighters then turned against Vortigern and stole his kingdom. We can't be sure if this really happened, though.

▼ The site of South Cadbury hill-fort, now inside a row of trees.

→ This illustration from a later medieval manuscript shows King Vortigern trapped in a blazing stronghold, having had his kingdom stolen by the Anglo-Saxons.

Hilltop battles

The histories mention several battles between the Britons and the Anglo-Saxons, when warriors fought to the death and local kings were killed. Archaeologists have discovered that someone built new defensive walls at the old hill-fort of South Cadbury at about the time of the Anglo-Saxon invasion, so there may well have been a battle there. On the site there was once a great wooden hall, perhaps where warriors met to feast and plan their fighting.

King Arthur's time

The legend of King Arthur probably stems from this mysterious time in British history, when heroic chieftains tried to fight back against the Anglo-Saxons. We don't know the true names of the heroes of the time, or any certain facts about their battles. One legend suggests that South Cadbury was Camelot, the home of King Arthur. Another says that an army of Britons left England forever and sailed away to France to begin a new life.

GO VISIT

South Cadbury hill-fort, Somerset

You can walk around many old hill-forts, including South Cadbury. Any buildings of the time would have been made of wood and have long since rotted away. However, the wood leaves behind holes in the ground called post holes, which can be used to work out the size and shape of the buildings that have disappeared. That's how we know there was once a hall at South Cadbury.

TOMB OF A KING

In 1939 archaeologists discovered a treasure-filled Anglo-Saxon burial under a mound at Sutton Hoo in Suffolk. It probably belonged to a local king who lived in the 600s. When he died he was buried inside a wooden ship.

→ After careful excavation, the imprint of a large burial boat was still visible in the ground at Sutton Hoo.

Rowed to heaven

Although the wood of the ship had rotted away, its shape could still be seen imprinted in the ground. The king's body had disappeared, too, but his treasure was left behind. He was buried with all sorts of objects that his followers thought he might need in the afterlife. There was even a purse full of gold coins for the dead man to pay the ghostly oarsmen who he thought would row him to a heavenly kingdom.

Fit for a king

The most famous object from the burial is the king's iron and bronze helmet, now in the British Museum in London. It has a dragon-snake creature stretched down over the top of the helmet, touching the nose of a dragon-bird with wings that make eyebrows, and a tail that makes a moustache. Also in the burial there were fine weapons, a shield and beautiful gold cloak clasps for the king to wear on his shoulders.

Who was buried here?

No one can be sure who was buried at Sutton Hoo, but from the dates of the coins in the grave historians think it might have been Redwald, a powerful king of East Anglia who died in the 600s. Redwald is supposed to have become a Christian, but his burial has pagan features as well. In his time, the Anglo-Saxons were just beginning to become Christian, but still using a lot of the old pagan traditions.

↑ The magnificent king's helmet found in the grave at Sutton Hoo.

GO VISIT

British Museum and Sutton Hoo, Suffolk

↓ A fine gold buckle for the Sutton Hoo king to use in the afterlife.

The Sutton Hoo treasures are on display at the British Museum in London. Replicas are in the museum on the site of the boat burial in Suffolk. As well as the famous helmet, the king was buried with weapons and a big shield. There was also a cooking cauldron, a drinking horn and a lyre (musical instrument). It seems he was expecting to dress, feast and drink well in the afterlife.

AN ANCIENT CHURCH

In the 600s the Anglo-Saxons began to build churches. A few of them were made of stone, and still survive today. Escomb Church near Durham is one of the oldest, from the time when the Anglo-Saxons first became Christian.

➔ Early Anglo-Saxon churches, such as Escomb, were kept very simple and plain inside.

⬇ The church at Escomb, one of the oldest in the country.

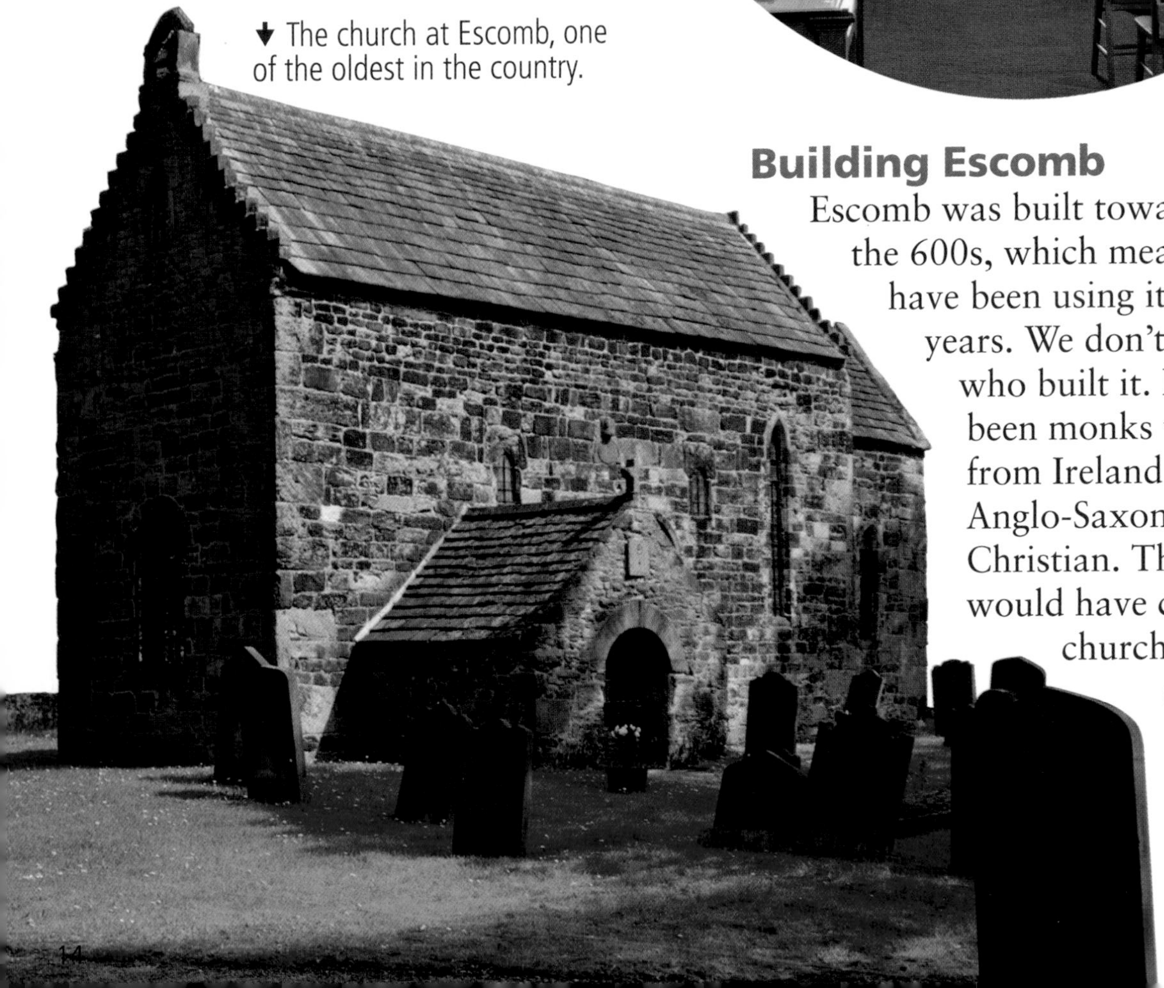

Building Escomb

Escomb was built towards the end of the 600s, which means that people have been using it for over 1,400 years. We don't know exactly who built it. It may have been monks who came over from Ireland to persuade the Anglo-Saxons to become Christian. The local people would have come to the church to hear Mass and to hear the parish priest preach to them about the Bible.

Roman recycling

The builders of Escomb Church used lots of ancient stones from the ruin of a nearby Roman fort. Some Roman carvings can still be seen on the walls, but we know that the Anglo-Saxon builders weren't interested in them because they put them upside-down or sideways. They re-used a Roman arch and even a door from the old fort.

Pagan animals plus prayer

Escomb has a very rare Anglo-Saxon sundial that shows old beliefs and new ones mixed together. It is marked with lines that represent times when monks prayed through the day, but it is also decorated with a carving of a serpent (a snake). The Angles who settled locally worshipped lots of gods, including a snake god, before they became Christian. Perhaps one of them carved this old pagan decoration.

GO VISIT

Escomb and other Anglo-Saxon churches

Check to see if any of the churches in your area were begun in Anglo-Saxon times. They might even have Anglo-Saxon treasures such as the very old carved cross found behind the altar at Escomb. It is thought to be even older than the church itself. One of the carved Roman fort stones reused in the church walls says 'LEG VI', which is Latin for 'The Sixth Legion'.

➔ The ancient stone slab from behind Escomb Church's altar.

WARRIORS RULE

In the 800s there were lots of local warlords, kings who controlled different regions of the country with their own bands of warriors. Evidence of their violent world includes a hoard of battle treasure and a wall of earth that once marked the edge of a warlord's territory.

↑ A glass stud with gold and garnets (dark red precious stones) around it. it was used to decorate something, such as a sword or armour.

The Staffordshire Hoard

In 2009 a huge hoard of gold and silver Anglo-Saxon treasure was unearthed in a Staffordshire field. It included fragments of finely made bejewelled sword hilts and scabbards and pieces of war helmet, as well as early Christian gold crosses. It may have been the spoils of war, items ripped from the bodies of dead warriors by the victors in a battle between kings. Nobody knows for sure who buried the treasure, but it may have been warriors from Mercia, an Anglo-Saxon kingdom that once included Staffordshire.

↓ The hoard lay not far below the ground in a farmer's field. This decorated piece has been put next to a modern coin to show its size.

Warlord kings

Mercia stretched across the middle of England, and was ruled by aggressive warlords in the 7th and 8th centuries. Offa was the most famous Mercian king, ruling in the 700s. He was a 'bretwalda', which means he was an overlord of other kings and one of the most powerful rulers of the time. To keep out neighbours he had a steep earth bank, now called Offa's Dyke, built along the Welsh border.

Hard fighters

A king would have had a band of crack warrior bodyguards called his 'hearthtroop', and also lots of other warriors he could call on to fight in his 'fyrd' (army) if he needed them. Warriors fought on foot, armed with a helmet, spear, shield and sword. They were fiercely loyal, and would fight to the death for their master. In return for their loyalty the king gave them land and gifts. It was a disgrace to survive on a battlefield after your leader had been killed, and you were supposed to keep on fighting to avenge his death.

← A gold and garnet-encrusted fitting for the hilt of a sword.

← Part of a golden dagger hilt.

Offa's Dyke and the Staffordshire Hoard

You can walk part of Offa's Dyke and visit an information centre about it at Knighton in Powys. It probably once had a wooden palisade (defensive wall) running along the top. When this book was written, the Staffordshire Hoard was still being studied by archaeologists but it is likely to go on display at a major British museum.

→ The remains of Offa's Dyke stretch across the countryside.

A MONK WHO MADE HISTORY

Once the Anglo-Saxons became Christian they began to build monasteries. The most famous Anglo-Saxon monk was Bede, who lived in Jarrow, Northumberland, in the 8th century. He wrote the first history of England and was the first writer to suggest the idea of England as a united country.

Boyhood of Bede

Bede went to live in a monastery when he was seven. Children didn't go to school in Anglo-Saxon times, but bright boys like Bede were sometimes sent to become monks. The monastery at Jarrow had a big library and Bede would have studied the manuscripts there. He would have learned to read and write Latin and Anglo-Saxon English, using a pen made from a bird feather or a reed.

→ A depiction of Bede, from a medieval manuscript.

GO VISIT

Bede's World Museum, Jarrow, Northumberland

The Bede's World Museum is on the site of Bede's monastery. There you can find out all about his life, and what it was like to be an Anglo-Saxon in Northumberland over 1,400 years ago. There are recreated buildings, a monastic garden and even an Anglo-Saxon farm. Remains from the monastery are on display, including stone carvings and pen nibs that monks such as Bede used.

← A stone carving from the monastery, showing birds in a tree.

↓ The tomb of Bede, in the Galilee Chapel of Durham Cathedral.

A monk's day

Monks wore a long robe called a habit, with a belt tied round the middle. They spent their days praying and working. Some would work in the scriptorium (writing room), copying and decorating manuscripts. Others would work around the monastery – on farmland or in the kitchens, for instance. They all worshipped in the monastery church several times a day.

Secrets of illumination

The monks copied out parts of the Bible or sometimes stories they knew. They decorated the writing with tiny beautiful drawings called illuminations. They stretched and scraped animal skins to make a yellowy material called vellum, which they used as paper. Then they made inks from ground-up rocks and plants mixed with egg white. Some inks were very rare and expensive.

A SAXON VILLAGE

Many Anglo-Saxons were freedmen, villagers who lived with their families and farmed small strips of land near their home. You can see a reconstruction of an Anglo-Saxon village at West Stow in Suffolk.

Hut for a home

A typical Anglo-Saxon village house was made from wood and thatch, with just a couple of rooms inside. It would be dark – windows were rare – and the air would be smoky because a fire was kept burning but there was no chimney. There were wooden benches to sit and sleep on (only wealthy people had wooden beds). A hole in the ground outside served as a toilet. Anglo-Saxons very rarely had baths, so they must have been quite dirty and smelly.

Living by hard work

Each family would have a few strips of land to grow crops, and a few animals to use for their meat, milk, skins and wool. Everything from ploughing to harvesting was done by hand. Then, when the busy working day was done, food would usually be a meal of flatbread and vegetable stew called pottage, with meat on special feast days such as Easter. If the crops failed in bad weather, the family risked starvation. There were often years of famine in Anglo-Saxon times.

↓ The reconstruction of an Anglo-Saxon village at West Stow, with houses made of wood and thatch.

West Stow Anglo-Saxon Village, Suffolk

At West Stow you can walk around reconstructed homes and see just how the Anglo-Saxon villagers lived. In the museum you can see some of the objects, such as this comb, that belonged to the people who lived in the area between 420 and 650. Anglo-Saxons were often buried with grave goods, favourite objects that they owned in life. These might be beads or brooches, tools or, in the case of children, carved wooden toys.

→ An Anglo-Saxon comb made out of animal bone.

Having fun

When it got dark, families sat round the fire by candlelight. They liked to tell stories, sing songs or make up riddles. They had board games, wooden toys and musical instruments including whistles made from reed. On special days, such as weddings, the whole village would feast and party together. Occasionally visitors might come to the village. A pedlar might arrive to sell things from faraway, or a messenger might come from the king's hall, with news of the kingdom.

A KING IN HIDING

At the end of the 700s a murderous new danger appeared that almost wiped out the Anglo-Saxons. Viking raiders arrived from Scandinavia, killing local kings and taking land for themselves. Only one Anglo-Saxon leader, King Alfred of Wessex, was able to stop them.

A secret hiding place

The Vikings conquered the south, east and north. In the southwest Alfred managed to stop their advance for a while, but in 878 a Viking army under a leader called Guthrum defeated him and he had to hide with a small band of warriors on the Isle of Athelney in Somerset. It was a tiny island hidden amongst marshes, reached by a secret route that only locals knew.

Alfred's legends

There are two famous legends about Alfred's time hiding in the marshes. The first tells how, while he was on the run, he took refuge in a peasant's hut. The lady there asked him to watch the loaves she was baking, but he accidentally let them burn. She told him off, not realising that he was the king. The second legend is that Alfred disguised himself as a wandering musician and went into Guthrum's camp to spy.

← The marshes around Athelney are now drained and there is a medieval church on the site of Alfred's hideout.

Victory at last

Alfred managed to rally enough warriors to help him defeat Guthrum at the Battle of Edington in Wiltshire. The Vikings then agreed a treaty that they would rule their own part of England, called the Danelaw, and leave Alfred to rule Wessex. He has become known as 'Alfred the Great' because he was such a hero in English history.

GO VISIT

The Ashmolean Museum, Oxford

At the Ashmolean Museum in Oxford there are lots of Anglo-Saxon treasures, including the Alfred Jewel, the most famous object associated with Alfred. It is made of gold and carved with an inscription meaning 'Alfred had me made'. It was probably the top of a beautiful bookmark, and it was found very near Athelney, where Alfred had a monastery built after his victory against the Vikings.

→ The Alfred Jewel. No one is sure who the figure is. It may be a representation of Christ.

A KING'S CITY

▲ A Victorian stained glass window celebrating King Alfred as a hero.

▼ This Anglo-Saxon dagger was found near Winchester in 1930.

Alfred ruled Wessex from the town of Winchester. He re-organised the laws and the army and he founded monasteries and schools. By the end of his reign the Anglo-Saxons were stronger and more able to defeat the Vikings.

Alfred's laws

Alfred was the first English king to have the laws of the land properly written down. Laws were strict and Anglo-Saxon punishments for crimes included drowning and beheading. Every free Anglo-Saxon had their own 'weregild', their worth in money, set by law. This was the amount of money that anyone who killed them would have to pay to their family. If the killer didn't pay, the family of the dead person could demand punishment.

Keeping out the Vikings

Alfred suspected that the Vikings would eventually attack again, so he built 30 fortified towns called burghs around Wessex. He also reorganised the army so that there were always some warriors on duty, ready in case of attack. He built new wooden ships for sea-going fighting, too. Some people at the time complained about how much he was spending and how much hard work he was expecting from everyone, but he made his kingdom much stronger.

GO VISIT

Winchester Cathedral and Museum, Winchester

↑ Winchester Cathedral was founded in Anglo-Saxon times, though the building mainly dates from later centuries.

Alfred's statue stands in the middle of Winchester, which he helped to build, and Winchester Museum has lots of Anglo-Saxon objects found around the town, including brooches, daggers and a beautiful bronze bowl (see page 9). Several Anglo-Saxon kings were buried in Winchester Cathedral, but not Alfred. He is thought to have been buried nearby but his tomb has disappeared, possibly destroyed during the English Civil War (1642-1651).

The learned king

Alfred thought that education was very important, and set up schools for young nobles. He ordered monks to start writing the *Anglo-Saxon Chronicles*, a yearly record of events in Anglo-Saxon England, and copies of the *Chronicles* were sent to libraries in monasteries around the kingdom. Nine copies still survive today.

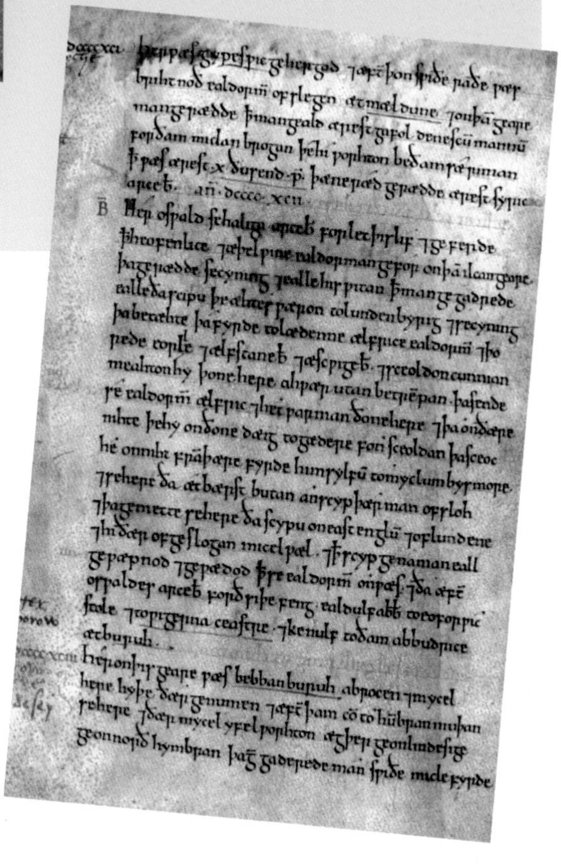

→ A page from one of the seven of the surviving *Anglo-Saxon Chronicles* that are kept at the British Library in London. The other two are in Oxford and Cambridge.

ONE TRUE KING

Alfred the Great's grandson, Athelstan, reconquered land from the Vikings and became the first true King of all England. He even called himself Emperor of Britain. His tomb is at Malmesbury in Wiltshire, once a busy Anglo-Saxon town.

Bloodthirsty battle

Athelstan claimed overlordship of Britain, but in 937 his Anglo-Saxon army had to fight off a huge invading force of Scots, Celts, Norsemen, Irish and Vikings. It was called the Battle of Brunanburh, though nobody knows for sure where it was fought. We know from writings of the time that thousands died on both sides and the victorious Anglo-Saxons chased the fleeing Vikings and killed them as they tried to escape.

↓ The town of Malmesbury in Wiltshire. Its abbey was important in Anglo-Saxon times.

Athelstan's town

Athelstan died in 940 and his tomb can still be seen in Malmesbury Abbey. By this time about 10% of English people lived in towns such as Malmesbury. Apart from church buildings there would have been streets, a market place and all sorts of craftspeople, including butchers, soapmakers and weavers. Boats would have sailed up the nearby river delivering goods from other towns and perhaps from faraway parts of Europe, too.

➔ The tomb of Athelstan, first King of all England. His bones are not in the tomb, though. They were lost years after he was buried.

GO VISIT

The King's Stone, Kingston-upon Thames

At Kingston-upon-Thames, near London, you can see the King's Coronation Stone. It's thought that up to seven Anglo-Saxon kings sat on the ceremonial stone to be crowned, including Athelstan. By the time of his reign, his kingdom was called 'Engla-lond' and the people spoke Anglo-Saxon English. We still speak lots of Anglo-Saxon words today, including such popular words as 'the', 'is' and 'you'.

Monks and monsters

Malmesbury Abbey looks different today because it was rebuilt after Anglo-Saxon times. But we know that it once had one of the biggest libraries in Europe and its monks were very learned. It's possible that a famous Anglo-Saxon poem, *Beowulf*, was first written down by a Malmesbury monk. *Beowulf* is an exciting adventure about an Anglo-Saxon warrior king who kills a monster called Grendel, and is finally killed himself while fighting a dragon. Beowulf is cremated on a funeral pyre as his best warriors ride around it to mourn him.

🡐 The King's Stone, where Athelstan and others received the crown of 'Engla-lond'.

THE LAST BATTLE

Anglo-Saxon rule came to an end on 14 October 1066, in a brutal fight to the death on Senlac Hill in Sussex. It was here that Harold, the last Anglo-Saxon king, was cut down at the Battle of Hastings and the Normans became England's new masters.

A double fight

Harold became king in January 1066, but two other people thought they should have the crown instead. One was Harald Hardrada, King of Norway, and the other was William, Duke of Normandy in France. In the autumn of 1066 Harold's army travelled north to defeat Harald Hardrada at Stamford Bridge. Just a few days later Harold's men had to rush back south to fight William's French invaders.

↓ A modern re-enactment of the Battle of Hastings. The Normans fought on horseback, the Anglo-Saxons on foot.

▲ The Bayeux Tapestry was commissioned by the victorious Normans to tell the story of the battle.

Horses versus shields

The Anglo-Saxons stood in a line on Senlac Hill and formed a wall of shields. Unlike the Anglo-Saxons, the Normans fought on horseback. They attacked from below the hill, repeatedly charging at the shield wall. For a long time it held firm, but eventually some Anglo-Saxons ran down the hill towards the Normans, mistakenly thinking the French were retreating. The shield wall was broken, Harold was killed and Duke William took the crown. Some Anglo-Saxon nobles tried to rebel but William saw off their challenges. He shared out English land between his French followers. Now the ordinary people of England had new lords to obey.

GO VISIT

The Bayeux Tapestry replica, Museum of Reading

The Bayeux Tapestry is a giant roll of linen embroidered with the story of the battle, from the Norman's point-of-view. The original is displayed in Bayeux, northern France, and there is a full-size replica at the Museum of Reading in Berkshire. In fact, evidence of the Normans is all around England because they began to build stone castles and churches that looked very different to those built in Anglo-Saxon times.

▲ Norman castles, such as Hedingham in Essex, were solid and imposing, very different from the wooden halls built by Anglo-Saxon nobles.

GLOSSARY

Afterlife Life after death.

Anglo-Saxons People who invaded England from Germany, Denmark and Holland in the 5th century.

Archaeologist Someone who uncovers, preserves and studies objects and buildings from the past.

Bretwalda Overlord of the country.

Britons People who lived in England and Wales before the Anglo-Saxons.

Burgh A fortified town built in Wessex on the orders of King Alfred.

Chronicle A written record of events. The *Anglo-Saxon Chronicles* were records begun in King Alfred's time.

Danelaw A part of England ruled by the Vikings in Anglo-Saxon times.

Drinking horn A drinking cup made from an animal's horn, often used by Anglo-Saxon warriors at feasts.

Dyke A long high bank of earth with a ditch behind it and a wooden wall called a palisade on top, built along the borders of some Anglo-Saxon kingdoms.

Eoldermen Anglo-Saxon nobles.

Famine Widespread starvation caused by bad weather destroying crops.

Fealty A promise of loyalty to a king and his nobles.

Freedman An Anglo-Saxon villager who owned his own land.

Fyrd Anglo-Saxon army.

Grave goods Objects buried with someone, for them to take to the afterlife.

Hearthtroop The bodyguards of an Anglo-Saxon king, made up of his best warriors.

Illumination A decorative picture painted on a handwritten manuscript.

Latin The language of the ancient Romans, still used for written documents in Anglo-Saxon times.

Legend A story that is not proven as being true history, but which has been told for centuries.

Monastery A religious building where monks live and work.

Normans Invaders from Normandy in France, who took over England in 1066.

Pagan Someone who worships many gods and goddesses, not the Christian god in the Bible.

Post hole A shape left behind in the ground when a wooden post rots away.

Pottage Vegetable stew, sometimes with meat added. The main meal of ordinary Anglo-Saxons.

Scriptorium A writing room in a monastery, where manuscripts were made.

Shield wall A line of warriors holding their shields in front of them to block the way.

Ship burial The burial of a body laid in a wooden boat. This was sometimes how important nobles were buried in pre-Christian Anglo-Saxon and Viking times.

Tapestry A picture woven from woollen threads.

Thane An Anglo-Saxon warrior.

Vellum Scraped and stretched animal skin used instead of paper.

Vikings Invaders who came from Norway, Sweden and Denmark in the 8th century.

Weregild A fine that had to be paid to someone's family if they were killed.

PLACES TO VISIT

Ashmolean Museum
Beaumont Street
Oxford, OX1 2PH
www.ashmolean.org/collections/

Athelstan Museum
Cross Hayes
Malmesbury, SN16 9BZ
www.athelstanmuseum.org.uk/index.html

Bayeux Tapestry Museum
13 rue de Nesmond
Centre Guillaume le Conquerant Bayeux
France
www.tapisserie-bayeux.fr/

Bede's World
Church Bank
Jarrow
Tyne and Wear, NE32 3DY
www.bedesworld.co.uk/

British Library
St Pancras
96 Euston Road
London, NW1 2DB
www.bl.uk/

British Museum
Great Russell Street
London, WC1B 3DG
www.britishmuseum.org

Escomb Church
Escomb
Nr Bishop Auckland
Durham
www.escombsaxonchurch.com

King's Stone
near Guildhall
High Street
Kingston-upon-Thames
Surrey

Malmesbury Abbey
Abbey Road
Malmesbury
Wiltshire
www.malmesburyabbey.com

Museum of Reading
The Town Hall
Blagrave Street
Reading
Berkshire, RG1 1QH
www.readingmuseum.org.uk/collections/index.htm
(The Museum of Reading has a Victorian replica of the Bayeux Tapestry. To view the whole of it online, go to: *www.bayeuxtapestry.org.uk*)

Offa's Dyke
Knighton
Powys
Wales
www.offasdyke.demon.co.uk

South Cadbury hill-fort
South Cadbury
Yeovil
Somerset

Sutton Hoo
Tranmer House
Sutton Hoo
Woodbridge
Suffolk, IP12 3DJ
www.nationaltrust.org.uk/main/w-suttonhoo

West Stow Anglo-Saxon Village and Country Park
The Visitor Centre
Icklingham Road
West Stow
Bury St Edmunds
Suffolk, IP28 6HG
www.stedmundsbury.gov.uk/sebc/play/weststow-asv.cfm

Winchester Cathedral
Winchester
Hampshire, SO23 9LS
www.winchester-cathedral.org.uk

Winchester Museum
The City Museum
The Square
Winchester, SO23 9ES
http://winchestermuseumcollections.org.uk

WEBLINKS

Here are some websites with information about Anglo-Saxons.

http://omacl.org/Anglo/
Get a taste of the *Anglo-Saxon Chronicles*.

www.bbc.co.uk/history/ancient/anglo_saxons/
Find out all about the Anglo-Saxons and try to identify their coins.

www.bbc.co.uk/schools/anglosaxons/
An Anglo-Saxon site especially for children.

www.spartacus.schoolnet.co.uk/MEDTsaxons.htm
Find out about the famous people who lived in Anglo-Saxon times.

www.regia.org
A site all about Anglo-Saxon life.

Note to parents and teachers

Every effort has been made by the Publishers to ensure that the websites in this book are suitable for children, that they are of the highest educational value, and that they contain no inappropriate or offensive material. However, because of the nature of the Internet, it is impossible to guarantee that the contents of these sites will not be altered. We strongly advise that Internet access is supervised by a responsible adult.

INDEX

Here are the lists of contents for each title in *Tracking Down...*

World War II in Britain

What was World War II? • Running the war • Defending Britain
The battles in the sky • Early warning systems • Air-raid shelters
Life on the Home Front • The children's war • Women in action
The war at sea • The Normandy landings • The end of the war

The Romans in Britain

Romans in Britain • People in Roman Britain • An army base
Busy Londinium • Britain gets roads • Soldier's town • Hadrian's wall
Roman baths and temples • See the show • A country villa
A mystery palace • Enemies from the sea

The Anglo-Saxons in Britain

All about the Anglo-Saxons • Anglo-Saxon people
Last stand of the Brits • Tomb of a king • An ancient church •
Warriors rule • A monk who made history • A Saxon village
A king in hiding • A king's city • One true king • The last battle

The Victorians in Britain

Who were the Victorians? • Queen Victoria at home • Running the country
Industry and manufacturing • The railway age • New ideas and engineering
Beside the seaside • Everyday life • Grand homes for the rich
Children and schools • Victorian health • Crime and punishment

The Vikings in Britain

All about the Vikings • Viking people • Lindisfarne • A great army
A Viking farm • A Viking town • Viking laws • Viking treasure
Shipped to heaven • Viking runes and art • Terror returns • Here to stay

Medieval Life in Britain

All about the Middle Ages • Medieval people • The White Tower
Harlech Castle • A manor house • Life as a peasant • Adventurer's Hall
Inside a priory • A cathedral • Medieval art
Going to school • Westminster Abbey

Tudors and Stuarts in Britain

All about Tudor and Stuart Britain • Tudor and Stuart people
Hampton Court palace • Reformation ruins • A dangerous tower
Disaster at sea • A grand house • A trip to the theatre
A busy kitchen • Civil war • A living manor • A monarch's cathedral

LS	6·10
LP	01/11
LF	08/11
LP	2/12
LP	9/12
LF	3/13